Unique Poetry for Adolescents

By Emma N. Wubbe

PublishAmerica
Baltimore

First printing

PublishAmerica has allowed this work to remain exactly as the author intended, verbatim, without editorial input.

ISBN: 1-60441-305-0
PUBLISHED BY PUBLISHAMERICA, LLLP
www.publishamerica.com
Baltimore

Printed in the United States of America

This book is dedicated to everyone I know or will ever know, to anyone who has ever pissed me off. If it weren't for all of you I would have nothing to write about.

Dear Readers,

I began writing poetry when I was in my early teens. At first, all of my poems were very dark. I was very depressed when I was younger and my poetry reflected that. As I got older my poetry started to reflect my interests, concerns, convictions, anger, sense of humor, and everything else in between.

As you read my poems you will notice that I have included explanations for each one. Some of these explanations will be short and to the point, others will be long and detailed, a few might offend you, but please keep in mind that these are my opinions, nothing more. I am not asking you to believe what I believe. I am just asking that you be respectful of my beliefs.

Happy reading!

Unique Poetry
for Adolescents

To My Mom

I miss you more each day,
I regret the words that I never got to say.
But I know you are free,
Far away from misery.
Please know that I love you still,
And I hope you are proud of my life,
As I still have time to kill.

Explanation: *To My Mom* is a short poem that I wrote to my mother a few months after she died of lupus in 2003. This poem is almost like a letter to her. I believe that the souls of those who have passed on can watch over their loved ones from the other side. I believe that my mother has in fact read this poem.

For Momma

Not a day goes by where I do not remember your smile.
Not a day goes by where I don't see your face,
Or remember Christmas' taste.
Your attitude was glowing,
It glowed like the sun.
It's hard to believe your life on earth is done.
I know you are in heaven smiling down,
And you see me,
Even when I act like a clown.
While alive you were are family's heart,
Even in death,
You still play the lead part.
On June 17th 2003,
Jesus called,
While your family bawled.
But we know you are now with the angels you love so much,
And we will always remember to keep in touch.
The battle you fought was brave and true.
We tried to be there the best we could for you.
Your body was beat,
And we hope you may now rest in peace.

Explanation: *For Momma* is another poem dedicated to my mother. Unlike *To My Mom*, which is more of a letter than a poem, *For Momma* is more of an "in memoriam". Although my views on religion have drastically changed since this poem was written, it still means a great deal to me.

I am of the firm belief that as long as you have faith and are a good person then you will be rewarded on the other side. It doesn't matter what you have faith in; my mother attended a Baptist church and was a kind and loving person, so I know she is happy and at peace. To me religion doesn't matter, purity of heart does.

Tragedy

Sometimes you can sense tragedy coming.
There is an unnatural calm all around.
It is like the first dark cloud,
Warning you before a summer's thunderstorm.
But sometimes you do not see it coming until it is too late.
It hits you unexpectedly.
Like lighting out of the clear sky,
And tragedy is upon you.

Explanation: I have had to face tragedy more than once in my life, and I am still very young. One thing I have always noticed is that right before a tragedy occurs or as it occurs everything is always calm. Three prime examples of this are:

1. The day my mother died. It was a beautiful June day. It wasn't too hot, wasn't too cold. There was a partly cloudy sky and a gentle breeze. Before that day my nerves had been on edge because I knew my mother was dying. I was on pins and needles waiting for that moment when I would have to say goodbye. Every other morning for months preceding her death I woke up feeling panicked, the first thing I would do in the morning was run to check and see if she was all right. But the morning she died, I woke up and I was calm. Even when my father knocked on my bedroom door and said the words I had come to dread, "Moms gone." I remained calm, collected and in control. I didn't break down until the funeral home came to take my mother's body, until my hysterical little sister was taken to stay with a family friend. It was as if somebody was there with me, helping to guide me through the most devastating day of my life.

2. September 11, 2001. Have you ever stopped to think about that awful day in American history? I mean really think about it, not just the attacks.

It was a gorgeous fall day, an unusually warm day in New York City. The sky was so blue it felt like you could see right into outer space if you stared long enough. I remember thinking to myself right after the second plane hit the World Trade Center, 'How could this happen? Today of all days.'

3. The 2005 London Bombings. I wasn't in London for the bombings, my best friend was. For her privacy I wont give you her name, but in July 2005 she was in London with her high school orchestra. From her hotel room she saw one of the bombings, a double decker bus exploding. A few weeks after the bombings when she was back home, we were in the middle of our weekly phone call when she said something that shocked me to my core, because it had happened to me more than once. She told me that while the rest of her classmates were panicking, she felt unnaturally calm. Like there was some unseen force guiding her. Her words, not mine.

All of this got me thinking, is there some kind of otherworldly force out there that guides us in times of trouble? I'd like to think so.

The Wolf

I feel the pain ripping through my body.
It makes me forget how to use my other four senses.
Makes me forget I ever had them.
Like tiny needles breaching every inch of my skin.
The pain is so intense.
As I lie somewhere between consciousness and pain induced slumber.
I can't help but wonder,
Will I one-day fall victim to the same wolf that claimed my mother?
Will I one day be forced to leave all those I love behind?
As I let fatigue consume me,
I think to myself,
The wolf will never get me.
The doctor said so.
But I am buying a shotgun just in case.

Explanation: When I was eleven years old I was diagnosed with a disorder called Fibromyaligia. It causes extreme pain flares that can be triggered by anything from changes in the temperature, to stress, to lack of sleep. One of my biggest fears has always been that I will one day find out that I have lupus, the disease that killed my mother.

Lupus is represented by a wolf in this poem for a reason, lupus is Latin for wolf.

My Depression

Can you find the light in the dark?
I can't,
I can only see that which is dark.
Asleep at night,
I find myself in an endless fight.
One might say you can hear life's spark.
I can't,
I can only hear the grim's bark.
I can see life's candle burning ever so low.
That which I fear is about to deal the final blow.
Some may call it a sick obsession,
I don't,
I call it my depression.

Explanation: As I said in the beginning of this book, I was a very depressed young teenager. I wrote *My Depression* in one of my darkest hours, when I felt like nothing would ever be all right again. I felt like my world was ending. Isn't it lovely the cheery thoughts a person can have when they are depressed? But let's be serious, depression is a very serious problem. If you read *My Depression* and it sounds like your life, see a doctor. You could very well be clinically depressed. On the other hand if you only have moments of depression every once and awhile, you probably just need to change a few things in your own life.

I am by no means trying to push drugs as a way to cure depression. I believe in exhausting every possible avenue of treatment before turning to medication. But I am not a scientologist, I believe in seeking physiological treatment if necessary.

Picture

Do you want to draw a picture with me?
But it is not just any picture you see.
It is a picture of my life,
A picture of my strife.
It is not drawn with pencil or pen.
It is not drawn with paint or charcoal.
It is drawn with a razor that bears my soul.
As I draw, a crimson river will appear.
As the river flows my troubles slowly disappear.

Explanation: *Picture* is about an epidemic amongst teenagers…cutting. Cutting is not pretty and it is dangerous. I myself did it for a while, so I know what I am talking about. Cutting is about masking pain, not creating it. Sometimes you can hurt so badly that you would do almost anything to make it stop. Cutters cut themselves so that they can feel physical pain instead of emotional pain.

If you are a cutter, you need to get help and fast. Tell someone you trust, that's what I did. I told my mother. If you don't want to tell your mom or dad, tell a friend, teacher, coworker, or call a help line, but tell someone. Cutting is serious, you could accidentally hit a vein and kill yourself. Get help.

The Castle

Spend a day in the castle from hell,
And dread will ring in your heart like a bell.
The castle has no discipline of faith,
It knows great evil,
But of what kind it will not say.
Enter the castle and your soul might not live another day.
The devil rules the castle like a mighty diplomat.
He stalks the halls like an unlucky black cat.
To know fear is to have spent time here,
In the castle.

Explanation: *The Castle* is my take on "hell", a place I don't believe in. I have a very difficult time believing the lake of fire scenario that is depicted in the bible. I wrote *The Castle* to show how easy it is to create a place people will fear. All you need is an imagination and a pen.

The Hollow

When you come here,
There is one place that you must never get near.
The hollow is not a place to be.
There are evils within that you cannot see.
Once in the hollow you can never leave.
Once inside,
By the hollow's rules,
You must abide.
In the hollow is nothing but dark.
I should know,
The hollow is my heart.

Explanation: I have already stated more than once that I was very depressed as a young teenager. I wrote *The Hollow* to show people how "dark" I thought my heart was. I used to think that my soul was very dark; I thought that something was wrong with me. But as I got older I realized that everybody has a part of himself or herself that they hide, a dark side. How many times have you thought something very dark and than said to yourself, "Where in the hell did that come from?" To me that is the dark side in each person.

The Dark Side

Deep in your fears he dwells,
Waiting to cast his evil spell.
He knows nothing of the light.
He is most at home in the dark, dark night.
He swims deep in your blood.
Sadness washes over you like the Great Flood.
You have no ark on which to hide.
But you must fight,
Fight the dark side.

Explanation: *The Dark Side* is about fighting depression. When I use the word "he" I am talking about depression. I thought I should tell you that because a few friends who have read this poem thought that I was referring to the devil when I said "he", I wasn't.

Judgment Day

We all knew this day would come.
We did not believe.
We did not see.
That the past would come back to haunt us in a dreadful way.
Now unsaved sinners must pay.
His Kingdom has finally come,
It is Judgment Day.

Explanation: *Judgment Day* is me making a mockery of the "End Of Days". To me the "End Of Days" is ridiculous because all the STORY does is make innocent people so terrified of something that may never happen that they turn to a religion that they may not fully believe in. That's what happened to me. When I was twelve years old a pastor sat me down and basically told me that I had to accept Jesus Christ as my Lord and Savior or spend an eternity in hell. I was told that when the "End Of Days" came I would be "Left Behind" if I didn't repent of my "wicked ways". If someone had told you that when you were a confused and depressed twelve year old what would you have done? Me? I got roped into a religion I didn't believe in and was stuck with that religion until I became old enough to realize that I had the right to choose what I believed in.

Oh the joys of growing up in the Bible belt!

What Do You Feel?

What do you feel when that sharp point hits your arm?
Do you feel pain?
Do you feel emotional gain?
Do you know that it can kill?
Do you even care?
Is the pain of life that hard to bear?
What do you feel?
My words cannot stop you,
Of this much I know.
But know what you reap you will sew.
Heed my warning before it is too late.
Don't take the devil's bait.

Explanation: I have watched more than one person in my life battle with drug addiction. *What Do You Feel* is a giant question to those people. I used to be so angry with them for being stupid enough to even try drugs. Now that I am no longer around those people all I feel is pity. Pity because they are living meaningless lives.

Use It

You don't have to do it you know.
Not even with your overbearing beau.
It's your choice,
You have a voice,
Use it!
No means no,
And saying it helps you to grow.
You are a gift,
If it causes a rift,
Forget him!
It's your choice,
You have a voice,
Use it!

Explanation: *Use It* is a warning to teen girls everywhere. I get really annoyed when I hear about sixteen year old girls who are no longer virgins. Girls, who are not old enough to understand sex, should not be having it. If you are not old enough to understand the consequences of sex, which include pregnancy, STD'S, and heartbreak than don't do it!

What Do You See?

Look at me,
What do you see?
Do you see what I am?
Or just what you want me to be?
What am I?
Who am I?
That is what you need to learn,
Why does my soul burn?
Who does it burn for?
If you picked that it burns for you,
Than you really need to learn.

Explanation: *What Do You See* is about not changing who you are for anyone. Be yourself, don't hide who you really are, find friends who love you for you. Never let anyone make you feel like you're less than him or her just because you won't act the way they want you to act.

Save Me

Please save me from this dark and lonely solitude.
I know I am hard to understand,
I have the most annoying attitude.
I feel like I am sinking,
Sinking fast in quick sand.
I know I can be slightly obtuse.
My ideals are hard to believe.
I know some would love to see my neck in a noose.
But please believe me when I say,
I want to see the bright light of day,
In a lovers embrace.
So I ask you this,
Save me with your sweet kiss.

Explanation: This is probably the only romantic poem that I have ever written or will ever write. This poem was the product of loneliness, nothing more, nothing less.

The Heathen

Does it make me a slut to find a man attractive?
Does it make me a whore to want to catch a guy's eye?
In your day and time,
My behavior would have been wrong.
In my day and time,
You hear about sex everywhere,
You can hear it in a song.
Does it make me a bitch to stand up for what I believe in?
Yes!
To you I'm a heathen!
I can't voice my opinion,
To you that is wrong!
I should just stay in the corner where I belong!

Explanation: This poem was written in a fit of anger one Sunday after church. That was the day I walked away from organized religion forever. I was sick of feeling guilty about everything I did. Everything I enjoyed was sending me to hell. Listening to rock & roll was sending me to hell, reading *Harry Potter* books was sending me to hell, watching Disney movies was sending me to hell, baring my mid-drift was sending me to hell, being a free thinking, independent woman was sending me to hell.

I am a good person, I treat others with respect, I am kind and caring, and I lead a good life. So please forgive me if I don't think that listening to Metallica and watching Snow White is sending me to hell. Please forgive me if I do not believe in hell. Sometimes I think that pastors and priests get off on making other people feel like dirt.

Less than Perfect

Sorry I am less than perfect,
Sorry I am not a saint.
I have made my mistakes.
But what I have done has made me stronger.
I have the drive.
The drive to survive.
The road I take may seem longer,
But I have the hunger.
My life is mine,
And mine alone,
Now all I have to do is make it my own.

Explanation: *Less Than Perfect* is about accepting that you are in no way, shape, or form perfect. Everyone makes mistakes, learn from them and move on.

Only Me

I see you everywhere,
I reach out my hand to you,
But you turn into the air around us.
Wait!
There is no us!
It's only me.
Sometimes it's hard to believe,
It's only me.
It used to be us,
Together constantly.
But now,
It's only me.
Wait!
There never was an us!
It has always been,
Only me.

Explanation: *Only Me* is the first poem that I ever wrote. To be honest I can't tell you what it means. To me it doesn't mean anything. It is not about any relationship I have ever been in because when I wrote it, I had never been in a relationship. When I wrote it I wasn't even old to be allowed to date. *Only Me* is the only poem that I have ever written that holds no meaning to me. The only emotional attachment I have to it comes from the fact that it was my first poem.

Think Before You Speak

Did I just say that out loud?
Oh shit!
I did!
Oh man, they are looking at me now.
A few look murderous.
That one girl with the pompoms looks particularly unhappy.
Why did I say that?
I didn't mean it!
Okay I did!
But I didn't mean to say it out load!
Why oh why did I say that cheerleaders are more hyper than kangaroos on crack?!
Okay time to run!
Note to self:
Keep inner monologue inner!

Explanation: I have a really bad case of foot in mouth disease. I say things before I think about them...it gets me in trouble sometimes. *Think Before You Speak* is my humorous take on that bad habit. And no I don't have anything against cheerleaders, this isn't a serious poem.

Betrayed

Two born of the same blood,
I trusted you.
You took my trust and abused it.
I once thought I could turn to you in times of trouble.
Now I run from you because you were the trouble.
Family,
What does it mean?
To me…everything.
To you…nothing.
You turned your back on me,
You sided with a liar and a cheat.
I was told not to trust you,
I didn't listen.
You betrayed me,
But in the end I betrayed myself.

Explanation: This poem was written about a family member with whom I no longer have contact. All I am willing to say about this poem is that it represents my feelings towards this family member.

You Lose

You said I was stupid,
You were wrong,
You lose!
You said I was lazy,
Wrong again,
You lose!
You tried to break me,
I was just a child,
You heartless bitch,
You lose!
I'm still here,
I am strong,
You were wrong,
You lose!
You said to cry was to show weakness,
I cry but it makes my skin thicker,
You lose!
You were there to teach me,
You didn't,
But I still learned,
You lose!
This is my game,
It's called my life,
I make the rules,
You lose!

Explanation: This poem wasn't just written with anger, it was written with pure venom. It is directed at my second grade teacher. I know what you must be thinking. Why as an adult is she still pissed off at her second grade teacher? The reason? I believe she is not only a bad person, but also an evil person. She never should have been given a teaching license. As a child I suffered from agoraphobia. I still suffer from a mild form. When I would have panic attacks, she didn't even try to help me. She made the attacks worse by glaring at me and telling me to be quiet and grow up. I don't remember ever receiving a kind word from her. She failed me that year saying I was a lazy coach potato. Coach potato my ass! I made up the year she held me back by skipping three grades and graduating from high school two years early. I was also a National Merit Scholar and I was accepted into a private creative writing college. Yeah I sure am lazy!

Do you know what angers me most of all? I wasn't the only child she did that too. The year she failed me, two other kids from my class were held back a year. Now even if she wasn't a bad person, doesn't the number of children she held back in that one year reflect on her teaching ability? I hate that she will never be punished for what she did. She retired or so I am told without so much as a black spot on her teaching record. Note to the wise: If your family can afford it or if your parents have the time, talk to them about private school or home schooling. If you don't have to go to public school you are better off. If you are stuck in public school hang on you will be out soon. Don't let anyone do to you what Mrs. "X" did to me. I was lucky my parents pulled me out of public school and I was home schooled after they found out what was wrong with me.

Public school screws over everyone, from the students to the teachers. And please don't get me wrong, I don't hate all public school teachers, just Mrs."X". I have all the respect in the world for public school teachers.

There is a learning store in Matthews, North Carolina where I have worked in the past. Day after day I watched teachers spend their own money on materials they needed for their classrooms that the state would not provide. I even worked with a few teachers who were there to earn extra money because their pay was so bad. They deserve respect.

I also want to give thanks to two teachers from my public school years who took the time and actually cared about me, Ann Dirr, and Sue Hooks.

If it were not for teachers like Mrs. Dirr and Mrs. Hooks, and all of the other teachers I met at that store, America's children would have no hope, God knows the government doesn't care.

Last Voyage

A maiden trip,
An average night,
Rich folk,
Poor folk,
All were aboard.
A chill in the air,
Ice ahead,
Ice behind,
Seven warnings at the bridge,
All ignored.
Now she rests on the ocean floor.

Explanation: *Last Voyage* is about a moment in history that I have been fascinated with since I first heard the story when I was six years old. *Last Voyage* is about the sinking of the RMS Titanic. The RMS Titanic sank on April 14, 1912 after striking an iceberg on her maiden voyage from Ireland to New York City. More than half of the passengers aboard were killed because the Titanic did not have enough lifeboats for everyone.

Phantom

Born into a world where you were unwanted.
A world where you were looked down upon because of something beyond your control.
You showed them all.
You became a legend,
An angel,
A ghost.
Your voice would haunt an opera house,
A child too vain for your affections.
For all your genius,
You could not see,
How great you were meant to be.
You lived your life in great despair.
But rest in peace,
The world knows your name,
Erik.
You are no longer just,
O.G.

Explanation: This poem is about a very heartbreaking story. This poem is about *The Phantom Of The Opera* and is dedicated to the man who wrote it, the late Gaston Leroux. When I researched the novel and discovered that is was not copyrighted, I knew I had to write this.

Gaston Leroux created a character so heartbreaking that it is hard to believe that Erik Destler AKA The Phantom is not a real historical person. So Mr. Leroux this is for you.

Monkey in Charge

You say we should listen to you,
But you never listen to us.
Hell, you never listen to your staff.
You hide away at your precious ranch.
While our sons, husbands, brothers lay down their lives in Iraq.
Our country is hated the world over,
Our economy is failing,
The founding fathers are rolling over in their graves.
You have poor grammar.
You have poor manners.
Why didn't we just put a monkey in charge?
It would have done better.

Explanation: Do I really have to explain this one? Come on, isn't it obvious what or who this poem is about? Well for those of you who are a little slow on the uptake...this poem is about President George W. Bush. I honestly think he will go down as the worst American president in this great country's history. Enough said.

Scotland: A True Wonder of This World

Deep and mysterious lochs,
Loch Ness where an ancient monster is said to swim.
Beautiful green glens,
Graceful highlands,
Scotland,
A true wonder of this world.
Imposing Edinburgh Castle,
A true site to behold,
Strong Scottish accents,
A mystical past,
Mary Queen of Scots,
Scotland,
A true wonder of this world.

Explanation: This poem is about Scotland…obviously. I am absolutely in love with Scottish history, folklore, and traditions. I look forward to the day when I can go for a visit.

The Lost Colony:
Croatoen

What does it mean?
Where did they go?
What became of the child with blue eyes and blond hair?
The first American,
Virginia Dare.
Did the natives take them?
Did they leave on their own?
Why did they never return home?
The questions are asked,
Year after year,
Decade after decade,
Century after century,
But we may never know,
What happened to them,
Where they went,
If they survived.
But the story of the Lost Colony is alive.

Explanation: This poem is about one of the most well known stories in North Carolina history. *The Lost Colony* is about the first settlement ever in North Carolina. The colony disappeared into thin air and was never found. A baby girl who was born into the colony, Virginia Dare, was the first child born on American soil. Because the colony was lost no one knows if she lived to adulthood.

Carolina Girl

Full of southern pride,
I prefer my chicken fried.
I like watching NASCAR,
What could be better than hot boys and fast cars?
I wear Daisy Dukes,
I love the General Lee,
Yes I know,
How much more country could I be?
It gets worse,
I have been known to yell and curse.
I like being barefoot,
If I didn't have to,
I would never wear shoes.
I listen to country, classic rock, and the blues,
I can say without a care in the world,
That I am a Carolina girl.

Explanation: This poem describes me to a tee. I have been called a "redneck" more than once in my lifetime and I am sure I will be called a "redneck" again sometime in the future. I love southern life, from NASCAR races to soul food. That doesn't make me a "hillbilly" or a "redneck". I actually prefer the term "southern belle". I am a Carolina girl and I am proud of it.

I Don't Believe

He came,
I believe.
He was a great man and healer,
I believe.
His blood was spilled on the cross,
I believe.
He died for you and me,
I don't believe.
God is real,
I believe.
God condemns non-believers to hell,
I don't believe.
There is an afterlife,
I believe.
Its called heaven,
I don't believe.
This poem will anger many,
I believe,
I'm going to hell for writing this,
I don't believe.

Explanation: I knew even before I wrote this poem that it would not go down well with many people. Hell, I'm pretty sure this poem won't go down well with members of my own family.

What will amaze you is that I AM a Christian. I am just not the typical Christian. Most people think of Catholics, Baptists, Methodists, Protestants, ect. when they think about Christians. I follow a sect of Christianity that you may or may not have ever heard of. I am a Gnostic Christian. Gnostic Christians believe in the teachings of Christ, but they do not believe that He died on the cross to save them from their sins. Some Gnostics debate on whether or not He even died on the cross. Some think He did, others think He was crucified but escaped death and went on to live a long life in France. But whether or not He died on the cross doesn't matter. I happen to believe he died. Gnostics do not want to make Christ out to be a liar or a false prophet. He wasn't, He was a real prophet of God. You see Christ never referred to Himself as the Lord and Savior. That was a title given to him after his death. Christ was a great man. I personally pray to him in times of trouble and worry and I pray to Him every night, he was a great and powerful man, more so than any other man to ever live. Gnostics follow his teachings but we believe He was a man, not "God With Us."

Gnostics also do not believe in hell. Why do we believe this? Simple, the books of the bible that refer to hell were almost left out when it was originally put together. If hell was real and so important to our faith, why were those books almost omitted?

Another reason we do not believe in hell? God is all loving; I and other Gnostics have a hard time believing that He would sentence His creations to an eternity in torment. God is divine, he is all loving, but he was given human faults, such as anger and jealousy by the penholders that wrote the bible.

Please bear in mind that these are only my beliefs. I am not telling you what you should believe. If Tom Cruise can believe that aliens founded the earth, than I can believe that Christ was not the Savior.

Blond; Not Stupid

I'm a blond,
But guess what?
I'm smart.
Not stupid.
I'm a blond,
But I don't support the market in rat-size dogs.
I'm a blond,
But I don't design over-priced pink handbags.
I'm a blond,
But I'm not a bitch, I'm nice.
I'm a blond,
But I wear cloths.
I'm a blond,
But I don't like to party.
I'm a blond,
But I have never driven drunk.
I'm a blond,
But I have never been to jail.
There are many blonds in this world,
But guess what?
Not all our names are Paris, Nicole, and Lindsey.
We make a difference in the world.
Don't you think it is time we were noticed?

Explanation: This poem is a below the belt shot at young Hollywood, I know. I have an intense dislike of Paris Hilton, Lindsey Lohan, and Nicole Richie. They set a bad example for young girls. Paris Hilton and Nicole Richie are famous for nothing. They are not talented and they don't seem to be very bright. Lindsey Lohan is talented but she was given free reign as a child star which lead to her drinking and drug problems. Young Hollywood needs to grow the hell up!

Pirates

Bottles of rum,
Crudely made cutlasses,
Walking the plank,
Wait,
They never did that.

Legends of buried treasure,
Pieces of eight.

Tortuga,
Jamacia,
Port Royal,
Their favorite hideways.

Blackbeard,
Captain Kidd,
Calico Jack,
Just some of the famous scallywags.

The Royal Navy,
Man of Wars,
Colonial Governors,
All brought an end,
To piracy on the seven seas.

Explanation: I love pirate lore. Living in North Carolina I have heard a lot of pirate stories over the years. North Carolina lays claim to the most notorious pirate of them all…Blackbeard. *Pirates* is just an ode to a fascinating time in maritime history.

Resurrection Mary

I walk alone in the dark.
In this cold and foggy place.
My heart is broken,
My soul displaced,
Some cannot even see my face.
Night after night I ask for rides,
Along the same road on which I died.
"Please take me home." I ask again and again.
Never knowing how many years it's been.
I was so young on that night in 31',
I was so young,
Yet my life was done.
So I'll walk alone on Archer Avenue.
Night after night,
As is my fate,
And you will lose site of me once we reach the Resurrection Cemetery
gates.

Explanation: This poem is based on my favorite ghost story. The story of
the vanishing hitchhiker, also known as the story of Resurrection Mary. I
wrote this poem to amuse myself one Halloween. Resurrection Mary is
the story of a young woman who was killed in a car crash. She is said to
haunt Archer Avenue in Illinois, the road it is said she died on. She asks
for rides from unsuspecting motorists and once the car reaches
Resurrection Cemetery she disappears.

The story is so popular that it was featured on the television series *Unsolved
Mysteries*. The story was also used as a plotline in the pilot episode of the
hit CW network television show *Supernatural*, even though the story was
altered a bit to make it a bit more frightening.

Grandfather Mountain

The highest mountain in the whole Untied States,
It truly is a majestic place.
A wondrous site for children,
The perfect place to go to cure summer boredom.
From the swinging rope bridge,
You can see below,
To a mountain ridge.
You can have a picnic up high,
Gaze out at the Blue Ridge Parkway with a sigh.
You can stroll through the small zoo,
One thing is for sure,
On Grandfather Mountain,
You will never feel blue.

Explanation: One of my favorite places to visit, as a child was Grandfather Mountain. Grandfather Mountain is the tallest mountain in the United States and is located in the mountains of North Carolina. It truly is a wondrous place to spend a fall day. The view is amazing. I remember when I was very little; I used to look forward to visiting the small zoo there so I could see "my" bear. Her name was Mildred. When she died when I was in elementary school, I spent a day crying.

If you have never been I thoroughly suggest taking a trip to Grandfather Mountain.

Fall

The leafs are changing,
The temperature is falling.
No more summer fun,
Fall has begun.

School is starting for a new year,
Children do not have many reasons to cheer,
Fall is here.

Hurricane season is in full swing,
The landscape is no longer green.
Two holidays to celebrate,
Thanksgiving
And
Halloween.

Explanation: I love fall. To me it is a welcome relief from the summer heat. I hate summer, but I adore fall because something about the season is just so…homely. I know it makes me feel alive.

Winter

Snow is falling,
Father Christmas will soon come calling.

Mistletoe and holly,
Everyone is acting jolly.

Shopping and wrapping paper,
The smell of pound cake is in the air.

Children are running around acting merry.
Uncle Walter is drunk and acting so stupid it's scary.

Christmas Eve is near,
Yep,
Winter is here.

Explanation: Unlike most people, winter is my favorite time of year. I am addicted to the holiday season. I love Christmas, a love I inherited from my mother. I have been told that I can be very annoying around Christmas time. I love decorating, baking, Christmas shopping, and pretty much being jolly…until I burn something or forget to get someone a gift…than I go a little crazy.

Spring

The weather is getting warmer,
The days are getting wetter.

April showers bringing May flowers,
What a joke.
More like April thunderstorms,
Bring May cleanups.

Tornado warnings,
Annoying severe weather news break ins.

Spring break brings bikini clad drunk chicks,
I have just one thing to ask,
Is it over yet?

Explanation: Spring is a time of year that I don't really like, but don't really hate.

While spring really isn't hot, here in the Carolina's it brings terrible thunderstorms.

I also hate "Spring Break". I swear for a week every year the bleach blond bimbos come out in force. Their sole purpose it seems is to drink as much as their size zero bodies will allow, while at the same time sleeping with as many men as possible. The scary thing is, these are college students. They are the future of this country. God help us.

Summer

It is blistering hot,
You're not sure if you will survive the season or not.

The city is in a drought with water restrictions,
So I highly doubt,
You will be filling up the swimming pool to stay cool.

Children are out of school for the year,
And parents are hoping the end of summer is near.

The Fourth of July,
Idiots with fireworks are burning themselves alive.

What crack head came up with notion of summer sun?
Remind me again why we looked forward to this time of year as children?

Explanation: I absolutely hate summer! I hate the heat that comes along with the season.

Almost every year here in North Carolina we hit triple digit temperatures and even air conditioners can not keep you cool.

I remember when I was little; I would look forward to summer all year long. Now that I am an adult, summer seems to last way too long.

I'm Not Hip

I am a young woman,
But I do not wear hip huggers and tube tops.
I was raised in the 90's,
But I am not overly concerned with money.
I don't like pop music, hip-hop, or R&B.
I don't feel the need to conform.
I don't like to gossip, shop, or text message,
I do not like fashion.
I do not follow trends,
I am original,
I think for myself,
I'm not hip.

Explanation: I have always taken pride in the fact that I am original. I do not follow trends, I never have and I never will. I loath today's fashion trends.

My advice to young women is…be original. Be yourself. You are unique…be proud of that.

I Thought You Didn't Judge?

The bible says not judge,
Yet you do,
Women's rights advocates,
Children's authors,
Gays,
Free thinkers,
And anyone different,
They are all worthy of hell in your opinion.
Children that are born,
Deaf,
Dumb,
Or,
Blind,
Are all being punished for the crimes of their parents.
Or so you say.
When you think about it all,
Those of you who judge are the ones worthy of hell most of all.

Explanation: This poem is dedicated to anyone who calls him or herself a Christian but acts otherwise. I hate people who say they are a Christian but than spend their free time boycotting gay celebrities and holding bonfires with Disney movies, *The Da Vinci Code*, and *Harry Potter* books as fuel.

The bible says not to judge yet I have rarely met a "Christian" who is not in some way judgmental.

You know there is something wrong with mainstream Christianity when bumper stickers that says things like. "The Only Problem With Baptist's

Is That They Don't Hold Them Under Long Enough" or "My Karma Ran Over My Dogma." are hot sellers.

If you want to call yourself a Christian please act like one, you give us real Christians a bad name when you don't.

Children Aren't Accessories

Do you understand what it means to be a mother?
How not to pass your children off to another?

Your kids are not some kind of red carpet accessory.
They are not a diamond bracelet,
They are not some kind of high fashion purse.
They are human beings,
Raising them is your responsibility,
Not a curse.
Grow up!

Explanation: This poem is dedicated to all the celebrities out there who allow nannies to raise their children. There seems to be a trend in Hollywood right now…having kids to boost public image.

The thing is I see at least half of those "image boosters" being raised by people other than their parents.

There are some celebrities I do have respect for. Angelina Jolie and Brad Pitt seem to actually care about their children. In fact whenever I see pictures of their children they are with their parents, not nannies.

Another couple I respect? Johnny Depp and Vanessa Paradis. They seem to take great care to keep their children out of the spotlight.

I want to make a plea to Hollywood. Stop using your children to get publicity. If you want to be a parent…be a parent.

Primetime

The new fall season is here,
The contracts have been signed,
The handsome no-talent teen idol has been given more money and will
stay for another year.

That show about vampires has finally been cancelled,
Its time slot has been filled,
By that drama about the superhero that cannot be killed.

The studio is hoping for an Emmy,
For that show about the crime fighting seer,
One thing is for sure,
I am keeping the TV off until after New Years.

Explanation: Okay, I admit it, I watch way too much TV. I have watched
television shows with all three of the plotlines featured in *Primetime*. I
wrote *Primetime* after spending a week on the coach sick with the flu. I
think I ended up watching every television show on the air that week.

I am one of those people who have the shows that they watch religiously.
On Thursday nights I can be found on the coach watching *Smallville* and
Supernatural, I rarely miss an episode of either one. And on Tuesdays I can
be found watching *Bones*.

While *Primetime* makes fun of well…primetime TV, I am one of those
people who watch it.

Mysteries of the Unknown

Ghosts,
Demons,
Grims,
Aliens,
Are they real?
Are they here?

Did you really just see that glowing figure in the corner?

What was that light up in the sky?

Are you just feeling evil or is something controlling you?

You just saw a large black dog, is your life over?

Are they real?
Are they here?

Explanation: I am a paranormal geek, a sci-fi fanatic. I wrote *Mysteries of the Unknown* for fun. There is no deep meaning to the poem.

Leave Me Alone!

I can't always be what you want me to be.
Leave me alone!

I don't always have the right answer,
Leave me alone!

I'm not always nice,
Leave me alone!

I don't always agree with you,
Leave me alone!

I don't always say the right thing,
Leave me alone!

I am not always happy,
Leave me alone!

I am not sad, just because I am not talking,
Leave me alone!

I am not always sick,
Leave me alone!

I do not always have a good time,
Leave me alone!

I don't always like your friends,
Leave me alone!

I am not always the perfect,
Friend,
Daughter,
Sister,
Girlfriend,
Aunt,
Leave me alone!

Explanation: Have you ever tried to relax only to have someone close to you ask you if you were depressed because you were not talking? That's happened to me.

Have you ever tried too hard to be perfect only to end up breaking down from the pressure you put on yourself? I have definitely done that…more than once.

When I wrote this poem I was at my breaking point. I finally said, "Screw It!". I was done trying to please everyone around me. It took me a while to understand that I didn't have to be perfect, that the people who love me will love me no matter what. I don't have to be everything to everyone…no one does.

If Life Was like Daytime

If life was like daytime,
I could drink in the middle of the afternoon and no one would care.
If life was like daytime,
I would always have perfect hair and makeup.
If life was like daytime,
I could be evil and people would still love me.
If life was like daytime,
I could murder my enemies and walk away a free woman.
Damn!
Too bad I am stuck in the real world.

Explanation: One of my guilty pleasures is watching my favorite soap opera, *General Hospital*, when I can find the time.

I have often watched the show and thought to myself, 'Why can't real life be like that?'. No matter what soap opera you watch, the characters always have it so much better than real people. No matter what bizarre drama that goes on in a soap opera, it always turns out alright in the end.

It is a pity that things never work out that way in the real world.

America

Red,
White,
Blue,
The stars and strips.
Where Old Glory waves,
Where the eagle fly's,
Where Lady Liberty stands watching over our harbor,
America,
Where freedom still rings.

Explanation: I am a very patriotic person. I love America. I hate our government, well more like I hate our president, but I love America. In fact I was first inspired to write poetry because I fell in love with the poem engraved on base of the Statue Of Liberty, *The New Colossus,* by Emma Lazarus. Emma Lazarus was a woman ahead of her time. In a time when women were not all that respected in the literary community she was able to write a poem that helped raise money for the base of Mother Liberty, her words are forever in the hearts of Americans. When I discovered I shared a name with a woman of such great esteem I felt overjoyed. To me only in America could a woman achieve such a feat.

Love Isn't Lovely

Love isn't perfect,
Love isn't easy.
Love isn't lovely.

Love is about compromise,
Love is about trust,
Love is about sticking it out through the tough times.
Love is about saying, "I love you", even when you want to ring his neck.

Love is about being able to turn to someone when you feel like the world
has given up on you.
Love is about having someone who will laugh with you, not at you.

Love isn't perfect,
Love isn't easy,
Love isn't lovely.

Explanation: I think this poem is pretty much self-explanatory.

I don't buy into the whole happily ever after thing. Life isn't perfect,
therefore love isn't perfect either. That doesn't mean love is bad. Love is
a great thing, it just isn't perfect. When you are truly in love it is the most
wonderful feeling in the world. But you do have those days when the
person you love is driving you nuts and all you want to do is throttle them.
That's normal. But at the end of the day there is no better feeling then
crawling into bed with that same person. Love isn't perfect, but it is one
of the best things in the world.

Bookworm

Nose always in a book,
Interrupt my reading,
And you will get at least,
A dirty look.

I enjoy learning,
When others find it boring.

It's a name I do not like,
Whenever somebody calls me by it,
I tell them to take a hike.

Yes I love to learn,
But please stop calling me bookworm.

Explanation: This poem is my way of trying to tell people that people like me, avid readers, do not like being called bookworms.

All my life people have picked on me because my nose is always in a book. I even have friends that like to call me "Hermione"…as in *Hermione Granger*, the know-it-all witch from J.K. Rowling's *Harry Potter* series. I really hate that.

If you read this and you are one of those people who make fun of "bookworms", please stop, its not nice.

Teenybopper Days

Boybands,
Pop Princess's,
Annoying earworm songs,

MTV specials that go on too long,
Pay-Per-View concerts that cost too much,
Please tell me I never bought into any of that?

Oh damn,
I did!

Thank God its over,
At least for me,
Those stupid teenybopper days.

Explanation: When I was between the ages of eleven and fourteen I was head over heels in love with the boyband N*Sync. Now that I am older, I look back on those days and wonder what the hell I was thinking. If you are still into the whole boyband/pop princess phase, trust me it will pass and you will be just as embarrassed about liking all that as I am now. But remember it was just a phase and everyone goes through it at some point.

It's Just a Crush

If he never looks your way,
Don't worry about it,
It's just a crush.

He isn't Mr. Right,
He isn't the world's most perfect man,
It's just a crush.

Sure he's good looking,
But is there more to him than that?
Is there any substance beneath that charming smile?
If the answer is no,
It's just a crush.

Explanation: This poem is dedicated to any girl who has ever been ignored by that cute, popular jock. It happens to all girls at some point in their lives. But word to the wise, that cute jock usually isn't worth your time. There are good guys out there, guys you might not even notice. Guys who aren't that popular, guys who might be complete goofballs. I've learned from experience that those types of guys are the keepers.

Please Shut Up!

You don't get your way,
Just because you are rich,
Please shut up!
You don't have a medical degree,
Just because you are a celebrity.
Please shut up!
You don't get to do anything you want,
Just because you are a pop princess,
Please shut up!
You are not above the law,
You are not God's gift,
So please,
Shut up!

Explanation: I really, really hate celebrities, well most celebrities anyway. I am a fan of a few of them. Gerard Butler, Jensen Ackles, Emma Thompson, Alan Rickman, Johnny Depp and Meg Ryan are all okay in my book. No, the kinds of celebrities I hate are the celebrities with God complexes. You know the ones who think they can do and say anything just because they are rich and famous. Paris Hilton who thinks the world revolves around her. And my personal favorite, Tom Cruise, who thinks he has a medical degree. Cruise pisses me off most because what he says could hurt people. He tells people that mental disorders do not exist because his religion (Scientology) says they don't. What if one of his fans who suffer from clinical depression, bi-polar disorder or something just as serious believes what he preaches and stops taking his or her medication and someone gets hurt? People with mental disorders do not always think clearly and could hurt themselves or someone else if they stop their treatment. If something like that does happen, I hope Cruise is held responsible.

Freedom of Speech

Freedom of speech,
It can be wonderful,
It can also be horrible.

It allows us to speak our minds,
It also allows wackos to be bigots.

It allows us to voice our concerns,
It allows big-mouthed talk show hosts to feel more important than they
are.

Freedom of speech,
Use it wisely.

Explanation: I am a fan of freedom of speech, obviously since I am
writing this book. But honestly some people take it way too far. In late
2006, early 2007 I refused to watch certain entertainment news programs
because I was so sick of reports about Rosie O' Donnell fighting with
Donald Trump. Freedom of speech is a gift that not everyone in the world
has so please don't use it unless you have something of value to say.

Days Gone By

Not that long ago,
Gas was cheap.
The economy was booming,
We had a president who knew what he was doing.

Not that long ago,
People could afford to live on their salaries,
Water was free,
Kids didn't spend so much time in front of the TV.

The days that have gone by,
Really need to return,
Before this country burns.

Explanation: I absolutely detest the state of America today. The economy is horrible, our president is an idiot that I wouldn't trust to run a vacuum cleaner yet alone a country, people cannot afford to live on the wages they are paid, and kids spend too much time in front of the television playing video games when they should be playing outside. Something needs to give before we end up living in a country of uneducated fools.

A Closing Word

Are you ready to leave this rabbit hole yet? A friend of mine once told me that reading my poetry made her feel like *Alice In Wonderland*. She told me that my poems went from one extreme to another and I guess my poems do, do that. I am a very opinionated person and I care about the youth of this nation. I wrote this book for teenagers because I know what it feels like to be alone, to be picked on, and to be bullied. I want anyone who feels like that to know, you are not alone and things will get better.

I know not all the poems you have read in this book have been serious. Some of them were written for fun, others were written about subjects that interest me. I hope you enjoyed reading them all.

Breinigsville, PA USA
08 November 2009
227243BV00001B/62/P